donation

A Life Science Wonder Book

# I Wonder What It's Like to Be a Spider

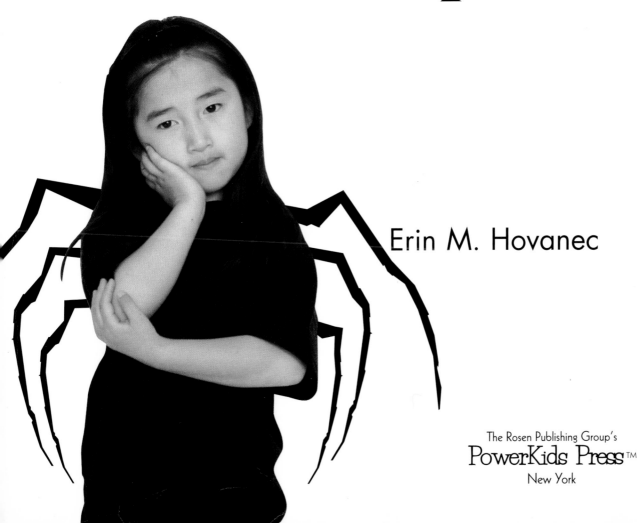

Erin M. Hovanec

The Rosen Publishing Group's
PowerKids Press™
New York

*To Joe—one of your favorite animals for one of my favorite brothers.*

Published in 2000 by The Rosen Publishing Group, Inc.
29 East 21st Street, New York, NY 10010

Photo Credits: p. 4 © IFA/Peter Arnold, Inc.; p. 5 © Animals, Animals/Zig Leszcynski; p. 7 © Hans Pflefschinger/Peter Arnold, Inc., © Animals/Animals/Ralph Reinhold, © Hans Pflefschinger/Peter Arnold, Inc, © M. & C. Photography/Peter Arnold, Inc.; p. 8 © Animals, Animals/Paul Berquist; 10 © Hans Pflefschinger/Peter Arnold, Inc.; p. 11 Animals, Animals/J. A. L. Cooke, OSF;p. 12 © Hans Pflefschinger/Peter Arnold, Inc.; p. 14 © M. & C. Photography/Peter Arnold, Inc.; p. 15 © Animals, Animals/Nancy Rotenberg; p.16 © FPG/Buddy Mays, © Animals, Animals/Michael Fogden, © Animals, Animals/Stephen Dalton; p. 18 © Animals, Animals/Rocky Jordan; p.19 © Animal, Animals/Bill Beatty, © FPG/Planet Earth Pictures; p. 20 Animals, Animals/ W. F. Mantis, OSF, © Ed Reschke/Peter Arnold, Inc.; p. 21 © Bill Beatty/Peter Arnold, Inc.; p. 22 © Jan-Peter Lahall/Peter Arnold, Inc.

Photo Illustrations by Thaddeus Harden

First Edition

Book Design: Felicity Erwin

Hovanec, Erin M.
    I wonder what it's like to be a spider / by Erin M. Hovanec.
       p.    cm. — (The Life science wonder series)
    Includes index.
    Summary: Introduces the physical characteristics, habits, and behavior of spiders.
    ISBN 0-8239-5453-6
    1. Spiders Juvenile literature. [1. Spiders.] I. Title. II. Series: Hovanec, Erin M. Life science wonder series.
  QL458.4.H68 1999
  595.4′4—dc21
                         99-29651
                           CIP

# Contents

# Spiders Are Super!

Have you ever wondered what it's like to be a spider, strolling around on eight legs and living in dark, dusty corners? Well, spiders do a lot more than just hang out in their webs. In fact, not all spiders live in webs. Some live in surprising places, like under water. Spiders are fast, sneaky, and they're some of the best hunters around. They also have the amazing ability to make **silk** that is stronger than steel. What would it be like to be a spider?

◀ *You've probably seen spider webs before, but can you imagine living in one?*

5

# Amazing Arachnids

Spiders have no bones. Imagine your body without bones. You'd be all floppy! Spiders don't need bones, though. Their bodies have a hard shell made out of **chitin**, a material that is similar to your fingernails. Spiders belong to a group called **arachnids**, which also includes animals like ticks and scorpions. All arachnids have a shell made of chitin.

Spiders come in all different colors. Most are black, brown, or gray, but a few are bright and beautifully colored. Most spiders have eight eyes, and all have a mouth. Above their mouth they have a set of sharp, pointed fangs. The most famous parts of a spider's body are its legs—all eight of them!

*Spiders come in all different colors, shapes, and sizes, but all of them have eight legs.* ▶

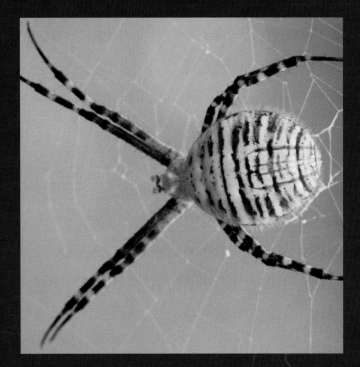

8

# Lots and Lots of Legs

Can you imagine trying to run, swim, or climb a tree with eight legs? If you were a spider, it would be no problem. Spiders' legs are very important parts of their bodies. They use their legs to find out about the world around them. Each leg has tiny hairs on it. Spiders use these hairs to smell and touch things. The hairs also sense movement and nearby **chemicals**, which spiders sometimes use to communicate.

Have you ever wondered why spiders don't get caught in their own sticky webs? It's because each of the spider's legs has a special claw on the tip of it. Spiders use these claws to hook onto the strands of their webs. Then they can swing around their webs without getting stuck.

◀ *Humans only use their legs to move around, but spiders use their legs to smell, sense movement, and swing on webs. No wonder they have so many!*

# Spinning Silk

Spiderman may not be real, but he's based on the real thing. Spiders really do shoot long strings of silk out of short, finger-shaped parts called **spinnerets**. Silk is a **fiber** that squirts out of the spinnerets and then hardens into a thread. Some spiders use that thread to build webs. Spider silk is the strongest natural fiber in the world.

Every spider has several different silk **glands**. Each gland makes a different kind of silk. Some glands make silk that dries quickly, and others make silk that stays sticky and gooey. Spiders can combine silk from different glands to make threads thick or thin, narrow or wide, sticky or dry.

*Spiders use the silk that they produce to build their webs.* ▶

11

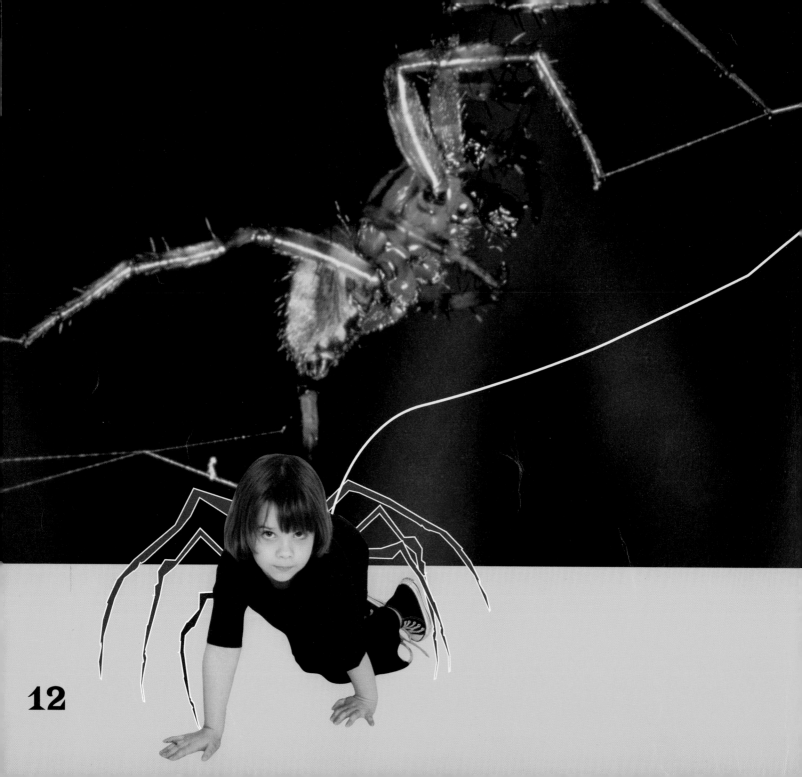

# A Spider's Lifeline

Spiders use silk for lots of things. They build their **nests** out of silk, whether they live in leaves, trees, on the ground, or in webs. Female spiders wrap their **eggs** in silk to keep them safe and warm until they hatch. Also, some spiders catch food with their sticky silk.

Spiders spin a silk thread behind them wherever they go. This thread is called a **dragline**, or a lifeline. When a spider is scared or in danger, it climbs up or down its dragline to escape.

◀ *Wouldn't it be great if you had your own silk lifeline?*

# Tasty Bugs

Spiders are fierce **predators**. Predators are animals that live by eating or attacking other animals. All spiders eat insects like flies and wasps. Some larger spiders also eat tadpoles, mice, small frogs, fish, and birds. These animals are a spider's **prey**. Prey are animals that are eaten or attacked by other animals. Some spiders even eat other spiders.

Spiders can't chew food. Their mouths can only suck liquid. Everything spiders eat has to be liquid. When a spider finds food, it spits juice on it. This juice contains special chemicals that **digest** the food and turn it into liquid. The spider can then suck up the food. Spiders are one of the only animals that digest their food outside of their bodies.

*Eating grasshoppers and frogs may sound gross to you, but they can be a spider's favorite meal!* ▶

**Spider preying on a grasshopper**

**Spider eating a frog**

A black widow spider

A hunting spider

A jumping spider

16

# Good Hunters

Some spiders, like tarantulas, are sneaky, smart, scary hunters. These spiders don't build webs to catch insects and other food. Instead, they hunt their prey. Hunting spiders have very good eyesight. They either sneak up on their prey or lie still, waiting for it to pass by. When their prey is near, they pounce on it, and then they eat it!

Some spiders leap on top of their prey. These jumping spiders can leap more than 40 times the length of their own bodies. That would be like you jumping halfway across a football field! Another group, called fisher spiders, are so light that they can walk on water. They dive underwater to capture food. Wolf spiders are so fast that they can outrun their food.

◀ *Black widow spiders, hunting spiders, and jumping spiders are all good hunters.*

# Weaving a Web

Although spiders have eight eyes, some can't see very well. These spiders spin webs to catch food. Many spiders build simple webs. Their webs are just a tangle of threads attached to a wall, corner, or roof. Dusty, dirty tangled webs are called **cobwebs**. Spiders called orb weavers weave the most complicated and the prettiest webs.

Spiders spin their webs very tightly, so they can sense even the slightest movement. No matter where the spider is, it can feel the entire web. That way, the spider knows immediately when a yummy insect lands on her web!

*Orb weaver spiders weave complicated and pretty webs.* ▶

Male and
female
orb weavers
and their web

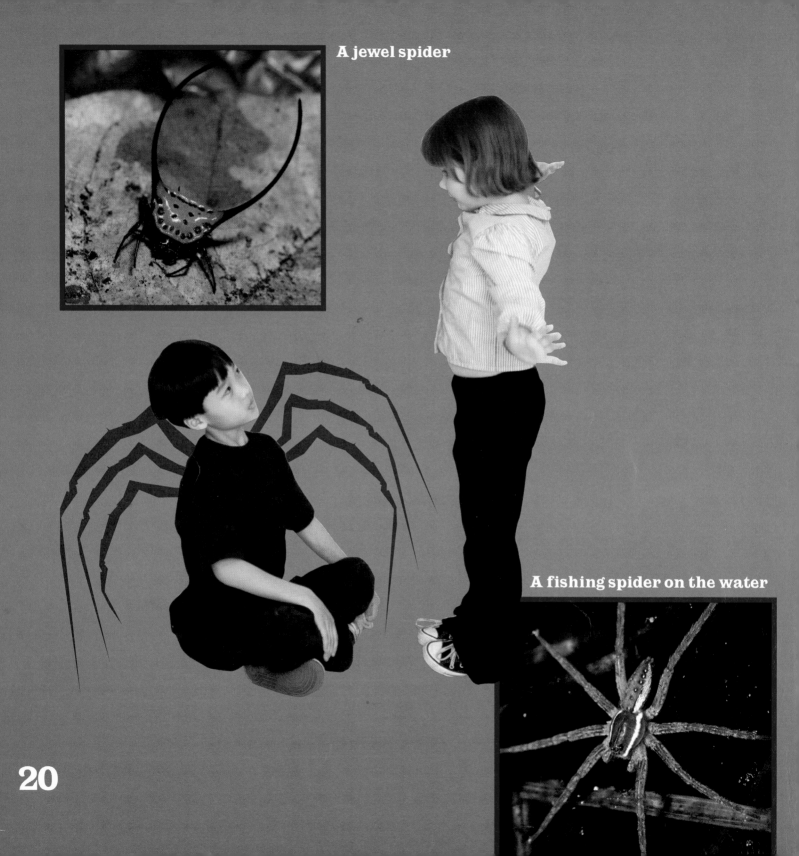

A jewel spider

A fishing spider on the water

20

# Finding a Home

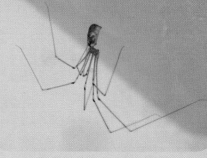

Are you sharing your home with a spider? Many spiders like to live where people live. They make their homes in houses, barns, garages, and other buildings. In fact, you can find spiders wherever you find bugs because spiders make their homes wherever their food lives. Spiders live all over the world except in Antarctica.

Spiders love snowy mountaintops and grassy fields. Some like dark caves, and others love sunny meadows. Some prefer dry, dusty deserts, and others call wet swamps home. Some even decide to dig tunnels and build nests underground.

◀ *Most spiders you find in your home are harmless.*

# Secret Spiders

Spiders come in all different shapes and sizes. They can be fat or thin, round or oval, short or long. Some are smaller than a pencil point, but the biggest spiders are bigger than a grown man's hand!

So far, people have discovered almost 35,000 kinds of spiders. However, **scientists** think there may be many more spiders out there. Some scientists say that there could be between 50,000 to 100,000 types of spiders in all. This means that many more spiders are hiding, waiting for people to find them. If you were a spider, where would you hide?

# Glossary

**arachnids** (uh-RAK-nehdz)  A group of small animals that have no bones and a segmented body.

**chemicals** (KEH-mih-kuhlz)  Substances with specific traits that cause a reaction when mixed with one another.

**chitin** (KY-tihn)  The hard material that makes up the outside of a spider's body.

**cobwebs** (KAHB-webz)  Spiders' old tangled webs.

**digest** (dy-JEST)  To change food into energy the body can use.

**dragline** (DRAHG-lyn)  Silk thread that a spider drags behind it wherever it goes.

**eggs** (EGGZ)  Hard shells that protect spiders before they are born.

**fiber** (FY-buhr)  A thread-like piece of material.

**glands** (GLANDZ)  Body parts that produce liquids for specific purposes.

**nests** (NESTS)  Homes that spiders build.

**predators** (PREH-duh-terz)  Animals that live by eating or attacking other animals.

**prey** (PRAY)  An animal that is eaten or attacked by other animals.

**scientists** (SY-un-tists)  People who are experts in the field of science.

**silk** (SILK)  A fiber that a spider produces that hardens into a thread.

**spinnerets** (spih-nuh-REHTS)  The parts of a spider's body that shoot out silk.

# Index

## Web Sites:

You can learn more about spiders on the Internet. Check out this Web site:

http://www.ufsia.ac.be/Arachnology/Arachnology.html